Thoughts that can change the life...!

-Meaningful words which inspire you

DEDICATION

To my little princess,

Manasvi

You are the light of my life, the source of my joy, and the inspiration behind my words. Your wisdom, even at such a young age, teaches me the true essence of life.

This book is for you—may it one day remind you of the power of words, the beauty of expression, and the endless possibilities that life holds.

FOREWORD

Every word and sentence in this book is deeply connected to life and the experiences I have encountered. Writing, I believe, is the best way to express our thoughts and emotions—especially in a world where people are often too busy to truly listen.

For years, these words remained hidden in my heart, unspoken yet ever present. It was my wife who encouraged me to bring them to life, to shape them into a book that might help others find meaning and reflection in their own journeys.

Happiness, I have come to realize, lies in continuous learning. Books, with their endless wisdom, never fail us—they uplift, guide, and inspire. If you, too, have something to express, I urge you to write. Your words have the power to touch hearts, change perspectives, and inspire others.

This book is not just a collection of words; it is a journey through emotions, experiences, and insights that I hope will resonate with you. May it inspire you to see life from a new perspective and encourage you to find meaning in the power of words.

{Dr. Mangesh S Jadhav}

PREFACE

This book captures a wide range of situations that people encounter in life. Some are drawn from my own experiences—moments I have lived and lessons I have learned. Others stem from observations, visualizations, and reflections on life's circumstances.

Written with the intent to entertain and inspire, this book encourages a positive shift in perspective. Words, when thoughtfully combined, have the power to shape meaning, evoke emotions, and transform lives. They hold more influence than any sound, as they have the ability to persuade, awaken realization, stir emotions, and redefine one's understanding of life.

Every word in this book carries its own story and significance, woven together to offer insight, inspiration, and a deeper appreciation for the power of language

Acknowledgement

If words are symbols of approval and recognition, let them serve as a herald of my deep appreciation.

I extend my heartfelt gratitude to my dear wife, Jagruti, whose unwavering support and inspiration have been the driving force behind my writing and the publication of this book. She is not just my support system but also my source of inspiration, sharing life's moments that transform into profound thoughts.

I am deeply thankful to my daughter, Manasvi, whose wisdom and understanding, even at a young age, teach me the true meaning of life. Her perspective continually enriches my journey.

My sincere gratitude also goes to my family, whose unwavering support has helped me fulfill my dreams. To my friends, who have encouraged me at every step, I am truly thankful. Each person who has crossed my path has imparted valuable lessons that have shaped my life in ways beyond measure.

Finally, with a heart full of reverence, I bow before God, my parents, and my well-wishers, whose prayers and divine love have nurtured me, both mentally and spiritually. Their blessings have been my guiding light.

Dr. Mangesh S Jadhav

Prologue

Words have power. They shape our thoughts, inspire action, and echo across time. A single sentence, spoken at the right moment, can change a life. From the wisdom of ancient philosophers to the wit of modern minds, quotations capture the essence of human experience in a few well-chosen words.

This book is a journey through the world of quotations—words that have stirred revolutions, comforted the weary, and ignited creativity. Each quote is more than a collection of letters; it is a glimpse into the minds of those who dared to think, dream, and speak with conviction.

However, quotations are not just relics of the past; they are living ideas. They remind us that history speaks to the present and that wisdom is timeless. Whether you seek inspiration, motivation, or simply a moment of reflection, these pages hold the voices of those who have walked before us, lighting the way for those who follow.

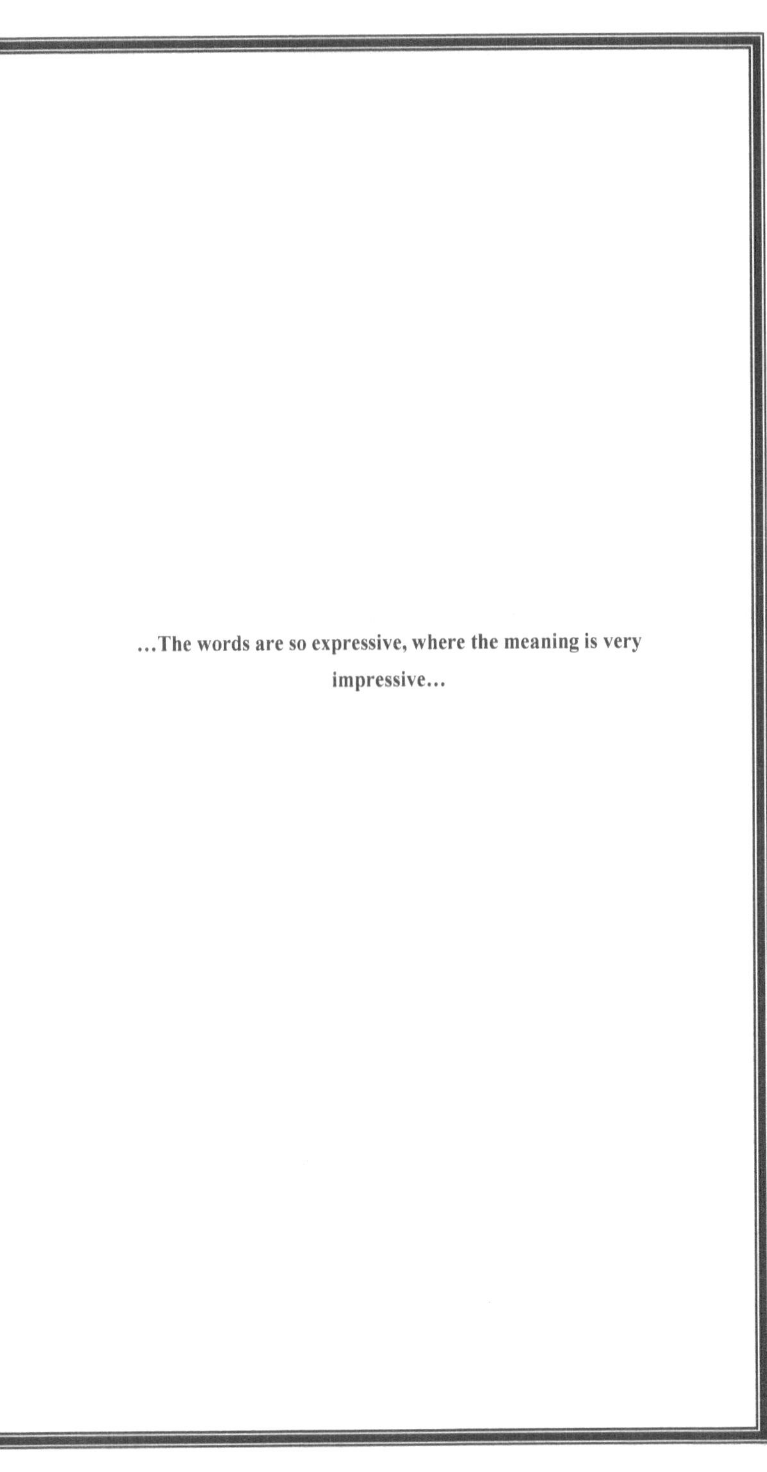

...The words are so expressive, where the meaning is very impressive...

It is so simple to be happy, but it is so
difficult to be simple…

Sometimes fight is between yourself,
be prepare to win…

Be ready for the next move with a
perfect plan…

Don't waste your valuable time with
valued person…

Observations going to teach you
many things than the vision we
have…

The people who walked into my life
made me better, and who walked out
of it made me amazing…

Going through worst situation is to
get best one…

Person who hides their feelings
usually care the most…

In the world of imperfection, there is
always someone who is perfect for
you…

Never feel regret for the thing you
did, rather to regret even though
when you have chance to do…

Many things in search of good people
we lose the real one…

The people who are strong enough
will never put others down, instead
they lift them…

Never announce your next move
before you make it…

Have the relation with the person
who hears you when you never said a
word…

We fail to understand the real value
of someone, until that someone
becomes memory…

In our life we are always bad in
someone's story…

Present yourself in such a way that, it
should not require any introduction…

In order to be strong enough learn to
face tough situation alone…

The strongest person is one who
makes time to help others even
though if they are struggling with
their own problems…

It's important to make someone feel
happy, and better to start with
yourself…

At some point life will make you
realize that the person can stay in
your heart but not in your life…

True relations are very hard to find
now a day's…

Complete your day with same hope
you started in the morning…

I believe in those who believe in
themselves…

A person with a fake smile in bad
situation is strongest one…

Helping hands will never rise to hurt
others feelings…

Finish your first chapter to start for
the next…

Build yourself in a perfect way to
develop others…

Helping hands are never tiered of
giving…

Affection with close ones is an
alternative to care truly…

Dark moments in life will open our
eyes forever…

Life with struggle and person with
trouble leads to success…

Innocence on your face, truth in your
eyes will win hearts forever…

Madness in relationship will make
bond enough strong…

Your first priority should be your first
preference…

Who knows about tomorrow, live for
present and be happy for a moment…

Step in of cute one in your life will
change everything you ever
expected…

In the life of colors be colorful…

Thinking too much on one thing will
stop you move forward…

Attitude will change everything;

show it in correct place…

A situation that doesn't take you to

destination is an experience for life…

A man with pure soul is perfect in all

the way…

Live the life you ever imagined of,

rather to leave it…

End is not about what you see in the

last but which is invisible…

Learn to be strong with weak

individual…

Take a moment to change yourself,
else some moment will change you
forever…

A lamp can be lightened in darkness;
a hope can be brightened in
sadness…

Too much attachment with someone
will make you stay alone someday…

Choose your own way for your
desired destination…

Dream to fulfill it in perfect time…

Our pocket doesn't decide who is rich
and who is poor where our character
does…

I am not always behind the things

which are not mine…

Face the difficulties in difficult time

to earn difficult one…

Be always expressive in all respect to

get positive response…

Be grateful to them who lift you in

your tough even though they are

facing from their own…

Happiness in your life depends on

quality of your thoughts…

Some people are always around you

but not close to heart…

Care for one who dares to share with
you…

Healthy arguments are far better than
unnecessary discussion..

Life is an art and we are the artist…

Play with the people not with their
emotions…

Every battle is not to win sometimes
to lose if it is with close one…

Think before you act, listen before
you react…

Commitment with your own thoughts

leads you to success…

Plan with determination to learn not

to win…

Motivate yourself to motivate

others…

Accept from unexpected one to stay

happy…

Nothing is going to take from you

until you give up…

Sometimes small conversation solves

big problems…

My struggling journey started at that stage, when I did not even know the meaning of struggle…

Create your own story by your presence; make your absence into a remarkable history…

A person with strong belief in himself is having courage for achieving the things…

Expressing oneself through the written word can give one a tremendous and unimaginable sense of power…

The sun watches what I do, but moon knows all my hidden truth…

One thing I learned in my life: No
matter how good you are, once you
will be replaced…

Sometimes we waste too much time
on thinking about someone who
doesn't even think about us for a
second…

All time smile on face, doesn't mean
their life is perfect but it symbol of
hope and strength…

Speak less than you know, have more
than you show…

Don't try about failures, worry about the chances you miss when you don't even try…

Try not to become a man of success, but rather try to become a man of value…

A creative man is motivated by the desire to achieve, not by the desire to beat others…

Every star deserves a chance to shine…

The secret of getting ahead is getting started to move on…

Love isn't something you find, but is
something that finds you…

Success is simple: Do what is right,
the right way at the right time…

Live each day as if your life had just
begun…

The difference in successful and
failures is not only the knowledge but
the lack of will…

Do well for others and luck will come
to you in unexpected ways…

The part of life lived for others is a
life of worthwhile…

We cannot become what we want to
be by remaining what we are…

We can't guarantee for a good day,
but can always face a bad day with a
good attitude…

Your achievements don't make you a
great personality where your behavior
does…

If you capable of learn something
new then it's not a waste of time…

Optimism is the faith that leads to
achievement…

If you are strong enough in your
determination of your desire then is
no option of failure…

People will always judge on how you
look, no matter how pure you are in
heart…

Life is not measured by the breath we
take, but the by the moments that take
our breath away…

I have my own commitment, where
sacrifice is only a choice…

Your future is in what you do today
not in what you do tomorrow…

Life is too deep for words, so don't
try to describe it, just live it…

If someone shows you their true
color, don't try to repaint them
again…

Take a deep breath; it's just a bad
moment or day not a bad life…

Sometimes the wrong choices bring
us to the right places…

When you start seeing good in others,
you discover the best part of
yourself…

Empires are not built in a day, have
patience…

Character is in how you treat those
who can do nothing for you…

If you want to be strong earn to enjoy
alone…

No reason to stay is a good reason to
go…

If you really respect someone, first
learn to hear what actual want to
say…

Even the smallest lie can break the
biggest trust…

Feelings are just visitors, let them
come and go…

If it doesn't open then that's not your
door you deserve for…

Before you start something, have a
plan of finishing first…

Be the love and respect which you
never received…

If you have a desire, then one day
you will at place where you wanted
to be…

At some moment keep your good
news with you, because not everyone
is genuinely happy for you…

It's really very hard to forget

someone who gave us lot to

remember…

The best view comes after the hardest

climb…

A few bad chapters don't mean your

story is over…

A eye with dust and a heart with trust

always cries…

Sometimes the person who made you

stronger is also your greatness

weakness…

If conversation with you is getting
shorter it means it is going longer
with someone else…

Its not about what you have in your
life, but who we have in our life that
matters…

It doesn't matter where you come
from, all the matter is where you are
going…

Dead people receive more flowers
than the living ones, because the
regret is stronger than gratitude…

Being ignored is the worst feeling
ever…

Efforts are better than fake
promises…

Two things to remember in life- Take
care of your thoughts when you are
alone and take care of your words
when you are with people…

When you forgive you heal, when
you let go you grow…

A sorry can never change the story
but gives relief to heart…

Stop waiting for the things to happen
instead go out and make them
happen…

Memories are like onion- they have
layers, the more you more peel, the
more you cry…

Your behavior becomes your
habits…

Learn to wait with patience there is
always time for everything…

When you help others, the universe
conspires help you…

Live in such a sense that you stand
alone today but tomorrow everyone
will follow your footsteps…

Behind every successful person, there
are always unsuccessful years…

Work until you have no longer to
introduce yourself…

If you can't sustain stress, then you
can't handle success…

When was the last time you did
something for the first time…

Live in such a way that, one day all
the people who didn't believe in you
will tell others, How they met you…

I try to be stronger because I have
faced everything which comes in my
struggling life…

I am strong enough to fight alone
than to explain others for where I am
right…

If you don't have enough confidence
in yourself then have confidence in
those who have confidence in you…

Be stick to your assigned work rather
to getting stuck in it…

In the world of imperfection, there is
always someone just perfect for
you…

People who hide their feelings
usually care the most…

When you truly love someone you
give everything you can and never
expect even in return…

Accept no one's definition of your
life, instead define yourself…

Best thing I did in my life believes in
me than any others…

Your future is in what you do today
but not in what you are going to do
tomorrow…

Don't be same as of others; just be
enough better that you can…

End the day with positive thoughts no
matter how hard things were…

Don't blame people for disappointing you; blame yourself for expecting too much…

In order to get the best one you have to face the worst one…

Be brave to stand for what you believe in even if you stand alone…

Really it's amazing how little tomorrow can make up for a whole lot of yesterday…

It's really better to learn to love the sound of your feet walking away from the things not meant for you…

Never to be too young to start an empire, never too old to chase a new dream…

People walk away easily but they leave their memories with us forever…

My brain is prison and my own thoughts are its prisoners…

First believe in yourself before you start and then you are half away there…

Revenge never works in our own power…

You are not enough rich until you
have something that money can't
buy…

Sometimes you do not write your
story, it writes you…

Don't die before your death…

The saddest people have the most
beautiful smile…

Be enough strong to face bad day
with a good attitude…

Its better to see something once than
to hear about it a thousand times…

Either I don't tell anyone anything or
I tell someone everything…

Where distance fails to separate the
relations, there silence does…

A mistake repeated more than once is
a decision…

Some are dying in the hope of getting
the love, whereas some are dying in
the hope of forgetting their love…

Remember you have to pay for every
story in your life…

Some stories are hidden within
yourself…

Other people never show difference
in relations where our own do…

For every problem there is solution
within it…

I may not better than other people but
I am different one…

To achieve dream you are not too old
or too late…

Mistakes are the growing pains of
wisdoms…

Don't lose the spark that makes
you…

There is something good in the life
and its worth fighting for…

Never stop believing in yourself, life
is full of miracles happens every
day…

Nobody can change a person, but
someone can be reason to change the
person…

Distance is nothing when someone
has desire to achieve you thought
of…

Switch off your ego and live from the
heart…

Be the love which you never received
from anyone…

Sometimes I feel that I need a break
from everything and everyone…

Kill the painful moments by creating
better ones…

I feel to stay away from everyone for
a while…

Be like a sun, alone but still shines…

If opportunity doesn't knock, just
build your own door…

A journey of a thousand miles begins
with a single step…

Take time to define your own path…

Your life is reflection of your own
thoughts…

If you can change your thinking, you
can change your life…

Never treat defeat as a failure, rather
treat it as a lesson…

When I look back in my life: I realize
the pain, mistakes & cheat, but I look
in the mirror I see strength, lessons &
pride in myself…

My life turned around when I began
to believe in myself…

See how crazy the world is: People are created to be loved and things are created to be used but in reality things are being loved and people are being used…

It's difficult to survive the life with the fire inside, than the fire around us…

Be the character like a sky where everyone aspires to reach…

Learn to sit back and observe, not everything needs a reaction…

I love people who gossip behind my
back, that's exactly where they
belong- behind my back…

Happy people are not grateful,
grateful people are happy always…

Real depression is when you stop
loving the things you love…

It's true that I am not perfect in many
things, but even this is true that many
things are not perfect without me…

The heart doesn't understand the
logic of people…

The most merciful person is the one
who forgives when he is able to take
revenge…

It is very easy to defeat someone, but
it very hard to win someone…

If we are not part of the solutions,
then we are the big problems…

If you are not happy being single, you
will never happy in a relationship…

In order to live satisfy life first enter
in your own life, love it and then
share it…

Kill them with success and bury them
with smile…

The biggest communication problem
is we do not listen to understand but
we listen to reply…

Don't be scared to be ALONE, goals
are personal…

Accept the challenges so that you can
feel the exhilaration of victory…

Love isn't something you find, but is
something it finds you…

Care is when the other person's
happiness is more important than
your own…

The great thing in this competition
world is not where you stand, but
where you are moving…

If you want to be successful one,
keep your eyes on the stars and your
feet on the ground…

If you work to create light for others
it means naturally you are lighting
your own way…

Happiness is not in accepting from
others it comes from our own
actions…

Best way to pay for life is to enjoy it
in proper way…

The person who defends you in your
absence is your true friend…

Difficult roads often lead to beautiful
destinations…

Personality is about who I am, but
attitude depends on with who you
are…

A good laugh and a long sleep are the
two best medicines to cure any
anything…

Better to stand for what you capable
of, it doesn't matter if you are
standing alone…

Don't afraid to give up the good for
the great…

Don't treat people bad as they are
rather treat them good as good you
are…

My life isn't perfect but I am thankful
for what I have…

My attitude is based on how you treat
me…

Sometimes you just need to hear how
much you mean to someone…

Don't focus on wound it scares &
hurts more, better focus more on
lesson which continue to grow…

Enjoy your own company than
expecting from others…

Never beg someone to stay with you
forever; it should be accepted not
invited…

The things which will never happen
again are the memories…

The best way to find yourself is to
lose yourself in the service of
others…

Value the person who spares time for
you because it not only time but he
shares the part of his life…

Nobody cares your story until it going to become a remarkable…

Never tell your plans, show them your results…

Be someone's light when they are hopeless…

You are enough stronger if you have been hurt many times and still showing smile…

The life in front of you is more important than the life behind you…

You ignore I wait, if I ignore you hate…

Don't worry of getting old, worry
about thinking old…

People will not realize the things until
it happens with them…

If it's perfect one, then it's not life…

Love is the most important but yet
confusing word…

Sometimes it is just matter of how
you see the things…

We are at the stage of life where we
are nothing but merely puppets of
time…

Perhaps it takes more courage to tell
the truth than harm someone to whom
we like…

Fear never goes away; just we learn
to face it…

We are so much obsessed with, what
other would think of it…

I don't care what people think about
me, but what I gave to them to
think…

Change your thoughts to change your
world…

If you want to be successful, you
have to disappear for a while…

Whenever I think of being quite,

situation makes me to speak more

loudly…

Involvement in work makes you to

learn more than expected…

The day I felt of taking rest after long

gap, life gives me some more

responsibilities to face…

It's more important to be important

for the important person in your

life…

Have courage to face everything you

come across…

As the patience ends from one end,
the close person becomes stranger…

Nothing is more important than our
own desire…

Respected everyone who disrespects
you to be respectful one…

Works ends with assignment and
starts with a plan…

Have a perfect plan to execute into a
remarkable history…

Play a game to win rather than to beat
opponent…

The memory plays an important role
in keeping relations strong…

People have always problems with
the others success…

Future comes from the way you live
today…

Nothing can be stolen until you hide
it with fear…

Be expressive to understand the
meaning of life…

I have never come across a struggling
life with easy steps…

My life is beyond imagination,
accepted without expectation…

Take a moment to bring someone up
than to feel them down…

Winning memories are not much
important than the failure one…

Competition with the competitor is
more important than the game…

Have a word to convince others but
not to confuse…

Having a confidence in you is almost
a way towards success...

Beauty is in the nature not in the
environment…

The things makes me active is my
own vision towards my goal…

Star is always in sky but we can shine
on the earth…

It is not true that all expensive things
are much worthy and important…

The pressure you create on yourself
takes you to rewind where you
started…

Solid things are not always strong
enough to be bold…

Slowdown in the relations is sometimes helps to rise in your character…

Accelerate yourself to move ahead with confidence…

The battle you fight is not only to win but to prove your strength…

Catch the memories you faced in the past days…

Chase your dreams to come with your attitude…

The blockbuster moment of the life is what you lived in and to whom you live for…

Contribution of the stories is mystery
for the future…

The order you follow is not always
being ahead…

Powering the dreams of tomorrow is
the efforts you make in present…

To secure your future is to stay with
your own thinking's…

Throw to hit not to beat…

Chase the titles with admirable
options…

Secret behind everyone success is much specific…

Something, somewhere, someone is waiting for you…

The attraction towards someone is not about beauty but it's of our own vision towards them…

The minds what think are always the eyes that see…

Attraction is not a part of intention, but acceptation…

The people who know your character, will not judge you on your looks…

Nothing is more important than the
loyalty…

The only way people will learn to
appreciate you is by losing you…

What will be your reaction, if you
meet right person at the wrong
time…

Work for the people who don't want
to see your success…

I regret for the things which I didn't
try where I was having chance to do
it…

I always intend to see real in people
than the good one…

Be the person to hold someone so
tightly that there broken pieces of life
with stick back together…

Sometimes it feels difficulty in
understanding my own feelings…

Be with the one who knows you are
not perfect but treats you as if you
are…

Work smart for something we have
passion of doing it…

Never ever announce your moves
before you make them…

Sometimes the best of your life
comes after the mistake of your life…

Silence is far better than unnecessary
drama…

Be with the one that heard you when
you never said a word…

Self education will make you a
fortune…

We never understand the value of
someone until that someone becomes
memory…

Once you feel avoided never disturb
them again…

Some people born to give more love,
whereas they know they will not get
in return…

We all are always bad in someone's
story…

Perfection is not achieved completely
by anyone, but if you keep chasing it
you will catch excellence…

The one who defend you in your
absence is true one…

It's better to lose people instead of
losing yourself…

I am waiting for the day when I am
able to say, 'I Made It'…

The best revenge for someone is just
being quite and move on…

A smart person speaks less and work
more…

Life gets easier when you ignore
those who make it difficult…

Sometimes you have to forget how
you feel and remember what you
deserve…

When you focus on the good, the
good gets better…

Don't wait for the opportunities to
come, just move on and create it…

Sometimes wrong decision takes you to right place…

Failure is moment not a life, so keep on trying till you achieve…

If someone doesn't appreciate your presence, make them appreciate your absence…

Find good in people and ignore bad in them…

Be a best listener, than a loud speaker…

When you make positive impact on someone else's life, it means you are

making positive impact on your own
life…

Everything in your life is your own
reflection…

Never expect anything from
anybody…

I always love to do the things which
people says I cannot do…

Solve the problem or leave the
problem but don't end the day with
problem…

Relation remains weak where there
are more doubts than trust, but it will

strong when we have trust than
doubt…

Life is not measured by the breath we
take, but by the moments that take
our breath away…

No one is more hated than one who
speaks truth…

Trust is what which takes years to
earn and matter of seconds to lose…

It is your life then define it
yourself…

One who wins without problem is
just a victory, but one who wins with
problems becomes history…

A beautiful life is a collection of
unforgettable moments…

Happiness is depends on your own
thoughts…

Always have faith in something
wonderful going to happen even
though of ups and downs…

Life will change only if are more
committed to your dreams…

It's so crazy how people are being
hated for real, loved for being fake…

Why is the person you want to talk
always hardest talk to you…

Be a reason that world should
remember your name…

Its true that nothing is going to stay
the same in the end…

Spend more time in living than more
time in worrying…

The best revenge you want to take is
improving yourself…

There are some pains which make the
person silent for entire life…

If you are remembered by everyone
then you are not ordinary one…

Most dangerous combination is to
think too much and feel too deeply…

The longer you hide your feelings for
someone, the harder you fall for that
person…

Your favourite song is so favourite
because there is some unforgettable
memory behind the lyrics…

Learn to say no before you need to
explain yourself before them…

The one dies from inside is pretend to
make others to live…

Don't let the behavior of others
destroys your inner peace…

Love your friends from your heart not
from your mood..

Don't regret for what happen in past,
rather make yourself a better person
to cover your past…

It's easy to leave someone, but it's
difficult to forget someone…

Sometimes the people who don't talk
to you are the ones that really want to
be with you…

Get strong to believe in yourself so
that others can believe in you…

Maturity is an outcome of repetitive
failures…

When you sit alone and thinks of
your past then you will realize the
way you have changed…

Smallest step in the right direction
ends up being the biggest step of your
life…

Don't need to accept by others you
need to accept yourself…

Sometimes you have to forget what
you feel and focus on what you
deserve…

You could had wait for some more
time, my time was bad not me…

Everybody deserves a second chance
but not for the same mistake…

If there is no way to move on, create
your own…

Strangers can become best friends
just as easy as best friends can
become strangers…

Punctuality is not in being on time
but to respecting our own
commitments…

When we are busy in earning money
the time is running behind us…

Replace negative thoughts with
positive ones you will have positive
results…
I need only true people around me
who understand me…

Only one person who can make best
decision in your life is YOU…

If it is not yours don't get too much
attached…

The last person in your mind when
you move to sleep is either reason for
your happiness or pain…

The worst distance between the two
people is misunderstanding…

Honesty is very expensive gift, don't expect it from cheap people…

Everything is real but not everyone is true…

Focus on possibilities than on problems you will find opportunities…

Before you start anything first learn to finish it…

Be ready for the new chapter in life…

Sometimes the questions are complicated and answer is simple…

One sided expectation always
destroys you…

Be with one who takes you as priority
not an option…

It's better to see once than to hear
several times…

A person who feels appreciated is
always work without expectation…

The person who cares you can
understand your silence…

Sometimes the wrong choices bring
you to right places…

People with worst past create remarkable future…

Being silence is a best response to a fool…

Open your eyes smartly before the life forced to close it permanently…

Think and use your words for someone you love, else your words can kill someone happiness…

Don't stop for a reason, and attempt to acquire it…
My pains in past and present are the greatest strength for the future…

Make use of proper time with proper
person…

If you care someone just show it, no
need to prove it…

Feelings can be controlled but tears
flows down…

Never have an permanent feelings for
the temporary person…

If you really want spare time with
someone just pay attention to their
words…

Focus on the people who inspire you
not the one who annoys you…

If you want to see who cares you just
disappear for a while…

Worst time teaches you many things
where even university fails to teach…

Be thankful to the past for
experience and lessons you
had in life…

A tear is an emotion where only few
can understand…

Sometimes we don't need advice but
someone to listen what actually I
want to say…

The best worst time of life is, we will
come to know who is really true and
fake…

Some people are cannot replace by
new one…

I think lot but very less expressive in
front of someone…

Never let someone to waste your time
repeatedly…

We mature with responsibilities not
by the years…

Don't compare yourself with anyone,
sun and moon has its own timing to
shine…

Sometimes I feel it's better to not to talk about anything to anyone…

Don't feel bad for ignorance, you are expensive and people prefer to buy only which they can afford…

Focus on solution instead of fighting for problems…

You are the only person who can make the best decision of your own life…

Don't run behind the one, who even don't care your presence…

Accept the end of something to begin
with new one…

Don't regret on your bad past, regret
on the time you wasted with wrong
person…

I respect the people who tell truth no
matter how bitter it is…

The pain you feel today is the
strength you feel tomorrow…

There are some voice which doesn't
require any words…

Respect for those who deserve it, not
for those who demand it…

A clear rejection is better than a fake promise…

It's better to be real than to be perfect…

I love listening to lies, when I already know the truth…

Take a chance because you may lose best but possibility of getting great…

Best memories make us sad, because it is going to repeat again…

The days that break you are the days that make you…

Memories return back but not the
time…

The hardest language to speak for
some it the TRUTH…

Without struggle we don't find any
progress…

Now a day's scaring moment is in
blindly believing people…

Don't show your dreams to people
just fulfill it…

If you are been ignored by someone
repeatedly, you too start the same…

The beats that make sound it the
rhyme of words…

Being faithful to someone is more
dangerous…

Do what you like not what you forced
to do…

What you see is not always real and
what you hear not always true…

The things get change when the
person stops trusting close ones…

Life takes you to the position you
deserve to be…

Trust keeps the relation stronger for
long time…

Once you stop believing in others
start believing yourself…

The things we feel attracts more than
the things we see…

I never find a faithful person a weak
individual…

Be positive in every situation which
leads you to successful one…

Work on the talent you will get your
destiny…

Be the bond which never breaks in
between for anyone, anything…

Wrong things happen when you trust
wrong person…

Never forget who helped you in
problem, while everyone else was
making excuses…

Sometimes keep your good news
with yourself not every time
everyone is happy…

If you want be great one learn to
forgive the people you love…

Face your fear else someone will
come and defeat you…

Don't easily judge me on my silence;
truth is in to understand my
feelings…

My life not perfect what I want to be,
but I am thankful for what I have…

Never lose the person who always
prefers to stay beside you at every
situation…

A random walk and random talk with
close ones gives you peace…

I am far away from the pain I had and
very close to peace want to…

I stopped explaining the people when
I realize that they are not interested in
listening…

The unsaid words will stay forever
with us…

Remember the person who makes
you smile just by being together…

Imagination is that which always
gives hope to live in…

It's difficult to sleep with plenty of
thoughts in mind…

It's hard to find someone who really
cares our feelings…

Complete your day with memories
but not with incomplete dreams…

Hugging someone is not about likes
and look but to be protected and
cared…

Never think of quitting the things,
just think why you started and for
what…

I want to meet myself by someone's
point of view…

Focus on what you to want in life not
what others think about you…

People with best advice are the one
who faced lot of problems…

I was somehow living my best life
and worst life at the same time…

Be with the person who stays with
you when you are alone, not he is
alone…

You will never understand the
damage you did to someone until the
same thing is done to you…

Time has a way of showing us what
really matters in our life…

It takes huge effort to forget
something you never want to be…

The only limits in life are the ones
you make…

Time has the way of showing us what
really matters in life…

Sometimes you should not react for
what have noticed…

Without change nothing would grow,
and without growth nothing would
survive…

Stay with someone who is proud to
have you in their life…

The person you fall for will never
leave you alone…

Hide your feelings from the one who
don't care about it…

Most expensive gift in this busy
world to spend your precious time
with family…

A person with true friendship is never
alone…

If life is a movie then we are the
actors, act to impress others…

The best inspiring person in girl's life
is her own father…

Every dream has own hidden story,
some tells some hides…

At the **END**

Never stop learning, if you do

so; Life will start teaching…

*****